MINING TO MINERALS

Design	David West
	Children's Book Design
Designer	Keith Newell
Editorial Planning	Clark Robinson
	Limited
Picture Researcher	Emma Krikler
Science Editors	Catherine Warren
	Michael Flaherty
Illustrator	Ian Moores
Consultant	Michael Stuart,
	geography teacher

© Aladdin Books Ltd 1992

First published in
the United States in 1992 by
Gloucester Press Inc.
95 Madison Avenue
New York, NY 10016

Library of Congress Cataloging-in-Publication Data

Clark, John Owen Edward.
    Mining to minerals : projects with geography / by John Clark.
        p. cm. — (Hands on science)
    Includes index.
    Summary: Describes various minerals and where they are found;
mining methods and machinery; and the need to conserve resources.
Features projects throughout.
    ISBN 0-531-17272-4
    1. Mining engineering—Juvenile literature. 2. Minerals—Juvenile
literature. 3. Mineral resources conservation—Juvenile literature.
[1. Minerals. 2. Mining engineering. 3. Mineral resources
conservation.] I. Title. II. Series.
TN148.C57   1992
333.8'5—dc20   91-34411   CIP   AC

Printed in Belgium

HANDS·ON·SCIENCE

MINING TO MINERALS

John Clark

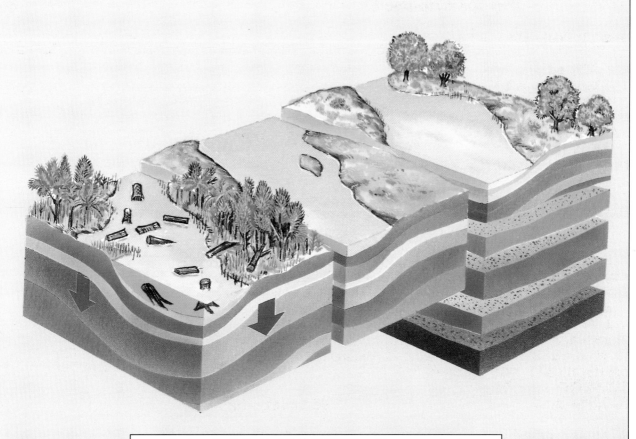

GLOUCESTER PRESS
New York · London · Toronto · Sydney

CONTENTS

Minerals are the nonliving resources of the earth. They include fuels such as coal and oil, metal ores, nonmetallic minerals like sand and gravel, and even gemstones. This book tells you how and where minerals were formed, and how they are obtained. There are "hands on" projects, using everyday materials and equipment.

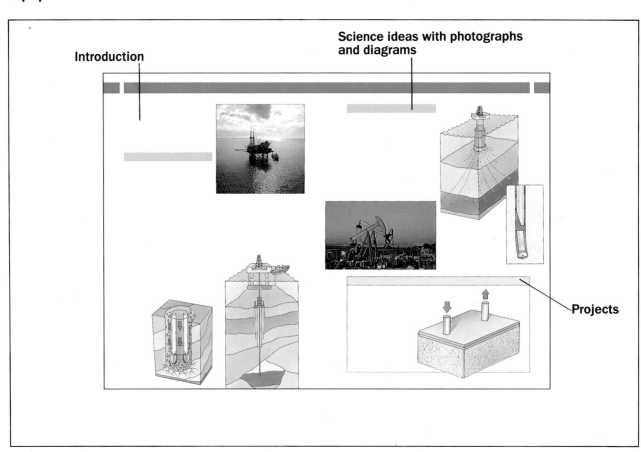

Introduction

Science ideas with photographs and diagrams

Projects

INTRODUCTION

Minerals are the building blocks from which rocks are made. A mineral itself is inorganic matter consisting of pure elements (the simplest of substances) or, more commonly, compounds of elements. Quartz, for example, is a mixture of silicon and oxygen bound together in a crystal lattice. Ores are naturally occurring compounds rich with substances, such as metals, that can be extracted or mined. Iron ore is a valuable mineral because it is used to make cast iron, which can be converted into steel. Nonmetallic minerals are used extensively in industry, agriculture, and medicine for such things as building bricks, cement, and fertilizers. Gemstones are also highly valued for their rarity and beauty and industrial use. But perhaps most valuable of all at present are the fossil fuels — coal, oil, and gas — which provide most of the world's energy.

A miner digs for opals in Australia.

The earth's crust contains about 3,000 minerals. Igneous rock forms granites and basalts. Erosion breaks these rocks down into sediments which may be compressed to form sedimentary rocks. Heat and pressure within the crust changes igneous and sedimentary rocks into metamorphic rocks.

WHERE THEY ARE FOUND

Minerals are found under the ground throughout the world, although certain types are concentrated in particular areas. Major deposits of oil, for example, are found in the southern United States and in the Middle East; the biggest reserves of nickel are in Canada and the Soviet republics.

These mineral concentrations occur due to formidable shifts of the Earth's crustal plates, creating ideal conditions for their formation. When molten rock, magma, from the earth's mantle bursts from the mouth of a volcano and eventually cools, rocks like basalt will form. Iron minerals come from water left over when magma cools. Seawater trapped within the earth's crust yields copper minerals. Where land-locked seas have dried up, evaporation results in compounds containing potassium and the sodium used in the chemicals industry.

Coal, oil, and gas, the remains of plants and animals, are buried where layers of sedimentary rock encased them millions of years ago.

Sometimes, because of earth movements or the action of flowing water, minerals are found at or near the surface. Gold nuggets, sulfur and even diamonds are unearthed this way.

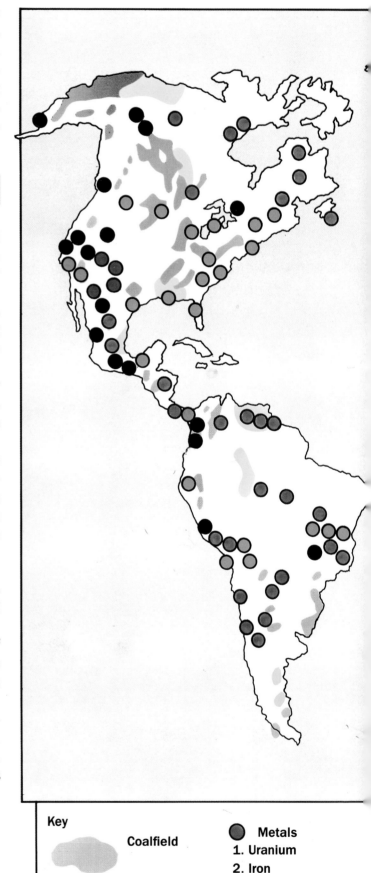

▷ The world map shows the location of the main deposits of metallic and nonmetallic minerals. The seabed and the oceans themselves are also major mineral sources.

Key

Coalfield

Oilfield

● Metals
1. Uranium
2. Iron
3. Manganese
4. Nickel
5. Copper

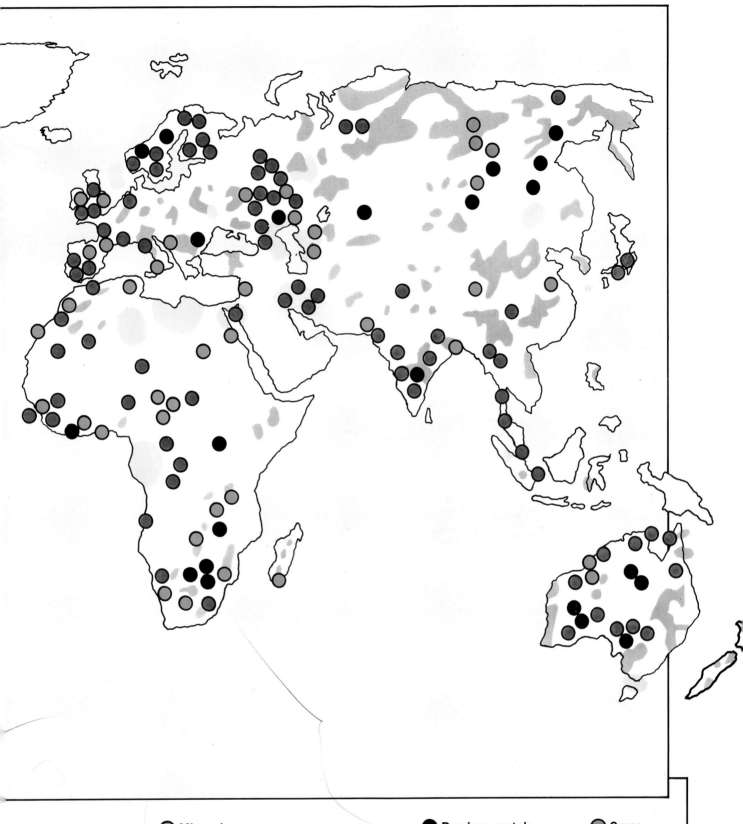

	Minerals			Precious metals	Gems

6. Lead
7. Mercury
8. Tin
9. Zinc
10. Aluminum

1. Asbestos
2. Clay
3. Mica
4. Talc
5. Borax

6. Nitrates
7. Phosphate
8. Potash
9. Rock salt
10. Sulfur

1. Gold
2. Silver
3. Platinum

1. Diamond
2. Turquoise
3. Emerald

Engineers use a wide range of methods to extract minerals, depending on their nature and location. Excavating machines scoop up the surface rock and sediment, so that useful minerals can be extracted. Shafts are dug and blasted to extract deeper mineral deposits. Wells are sunk to reach deposits of gas and oil.

EXCAVATING

Mechanical excavators of all types extract minerals that occur near the surface, such as gravel, sand, and many coal deposits. Digger excavators remove fairly small quantities of minerals at a time but are very maneuverable machines. Dragline excavators scoop up much larger amounts. They have a long derrick, or boom, which drops a large, toothed scoop. Steel cables haul in the scoop to scrape up soil, rocks, or minerals (see picture, page 30). Most complex of all are the huge bucket-wheel excavators. They have the largest capacity, moving up and down surface deposits very slowly.

△ A large bucket-wheel excavator scoops up coal at extremely high speed at an open-pit mine.

DRILLING

Drilling is used to reach deep deposits of nonmetallic minerals that can rise to the surface as gases or liquids. The underground pressure of natural gas, for instance, is enough to force it to the surface and along pipes to storage tanks. Oil may also rise under its own pressure, or is mechanically pumped to the surface (see pages 14-15). Gas and oil may be located on land, in shallow waters offshore or — using floating rigs — in deep water. Sulfur is extracted by drilling once the deposit is melted with pressurized hot water. It is also a by-product of the purification of natural gas.

△ Oil and natural gas production rigs are familiar sights in the shallow seas off the coasts of western Europe and around North America.

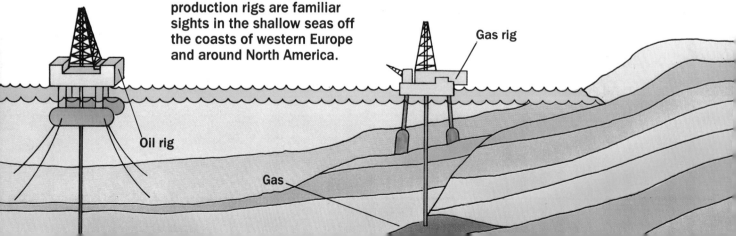

Oil rig

Gas rig

Gas

MINING

Minerals extracted by mining include coal, some gemstones, and most metal ores. The principal methods are strip or open-pit mining for pit deposits that lie near the surface, and underground mining for deposits located underground. Underground, engineers use blasting explosives to smash through hard rock to make shafts and tunnels. They also employ tunneling machines with mechanical shearers to extract the minerals. Conveyor belts, railways and elevators shift the mined material to the surface from where it can be transported for refining or immediate use.

△ An automatic shearing machine slowly moves forward as it continuously cuts coal at an underground coalface.

△ A powerful explosion frees tons of rock for building material in this blast at a large quarry.

QUARRYING

Quarrying is employed for surface deposits of hard nonmetallic minerals such as limestone, marble and slate. Instead of excavators, blasting explosives and deep cutting machines shape quarries, which resemble open-pit mines. Sand, clay, and gravel pits may also be regarded as quarries that do employ excavators and dredgers. In a china clay quarry, for example, the mineral is "excavated" using high-pressure jets of water.

▽ Mineral deposits occur in every possible location. The diagram below shows just a few of the methods devised for their extraction.

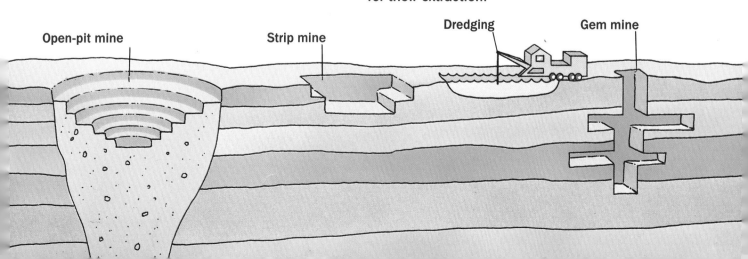

Open-pit mine   Strip mine   Dredging   Gem mine

Coal, oil, and natural gas are fossil fuels, so called because they were formed over millions of years from dead plants and animals buried under sediment. Lack of oxygen prevented the material from fully decomposing so that only the carbon or hydrocarbons (compounds of carbon and hydrogen) remained.

COAL

Coal, which is made of carbon, hydrogen, and oxygen, consists of the remains of plants that grew about 300 million years ago. When the plants died they sank below the water. Initially plant matter rotted down into a brown, fibrous substance called peat. Mud and silt covered the peat, depriving it of oxygen and preventing further decomposition. Pressure from successive layers of sediment changed the peat into lignite, or brown coal, and then bituminous coal as the compression squeezed out more hydrogen and oxygen. With sufficient heat and pressure, anthracite is formed, which is almost completely carbon.

△ A fossil of a fern found in a lump of coal indicates that ferns were common plants growing on earth when the raw material for coal was originally laid down.

▽ The formation of coal took place in stages over millions of years as dead plant material became covered in sediments and was gradually changed by heat and pressure. Peat is changed least and anthracite is changed most.

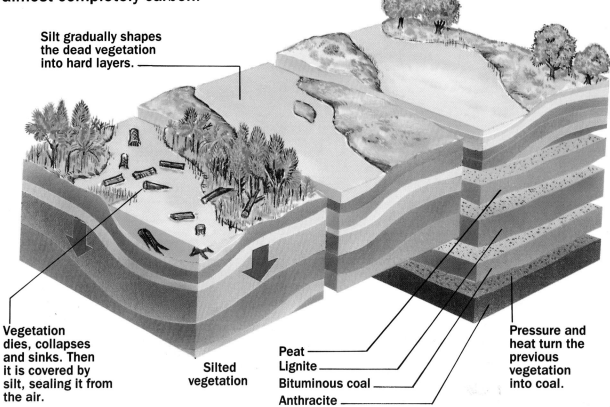

Silt gradually shapes the dead vegetation into hard layers.

Vegetation dies, collapses and sinks. Then it is covered by silt, sealing it from the air.

Silted vegetation

Peat
Lignite
Bituminous coal
Anthracite

Pressure and heat turn the previous vegetation into coal.

OIL AND GAS

Crude oil, also called petroleum, is a dark, sticky mixture of liquid hydrocarbons. Natural gas consists of light, colorless hydrocarbons. Both minerals were formed millions of years ago when dead plankton, the microscopic plants and animals that live at the surface of the sea, sank to the bottom. Covered by clay, silt, and sediment, the plankton remains were deprived of oxygen and did not rot. Further layers on top compressed this organic material, the action of pressure and heat transforming it to oil and gas.

Oil and gas can move through porous rocks and tend to move upward through consecutive porous layers. Eventually, they come to an impervious rock layer named a "cap rock." The oil and gas collect in the porous rock below the cap rock like water in a sponge. This is known as a trap. The oil and gas are extracted by sinking a well down into the trap.

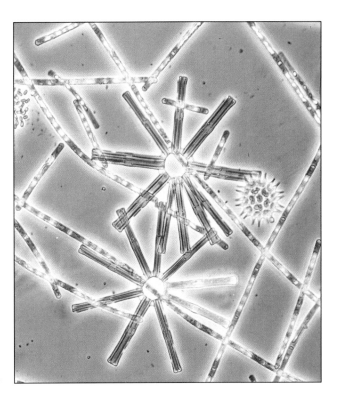

△ Microscopic plants and animals in plankton resemble the creatures whose remains formed natural gas and oil millions of years ago.

▽ Oil was formed in a similar way to coal. But oil is sensitive to heat changes within the earth. Oil will decompose producing gas and carbon if heated above 300 degrees F.

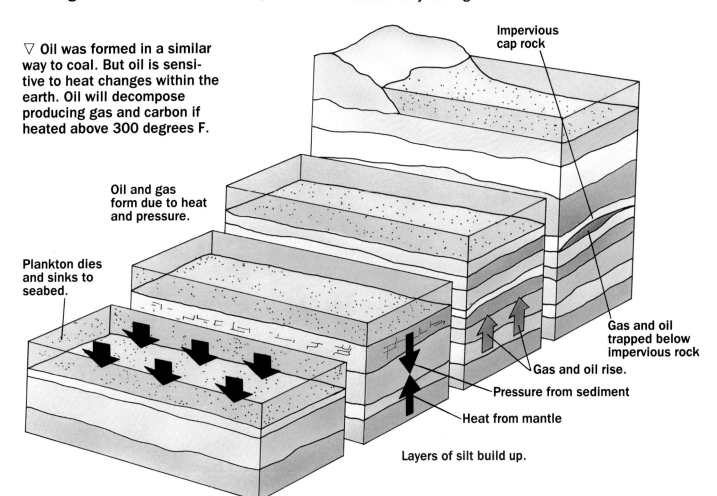

Impervious cap rock

Oil and gas form due to heat and pressure.

Plankton dies and sinks to seabed.

Gas and oil trapped below impervious rock

Gas and oil rise.

Pressure from sediment

Heat from mantle

Layers of silt build up.

Coal occurs at various depths in layers called seams. It may be near the surface, under a layer of soil. Or it may lie deep in the ground, under layers of sedimentary rocks such as sandstone and shale. Shallow deposits are obtained by open-pit mining; to reach deep deposits may need tunnels several miles long.

UNDERGROUND MINING

An underground mine has one or more shafts cut down to the coal seams. From a shaft, miners bore tunnels into the coal seams. Pit props hold up the roofs of the tunnels. In a modern underground mine (below), miners use automatic and semi-automatic coal shearers that slice off layers of coal at a high rate. Hydraulic pit props are moved forward as coal is removed. Conveyor belts and electric trains remove the coal to elevator shafts that bring the coal to the surface. Despite increasing automation, coal mines in China and India still rely heavily on manual work.

△ The winding gear at the surface is characteristic of coal mines. The gear works an elevator that hauls up trucks of coal and carries miners to and from the coalface.

▽ A mechanical coal shearer (inset) has rotating picks that chop coal from the coalface and load it onto a conveyor which carries it along a tunnel.

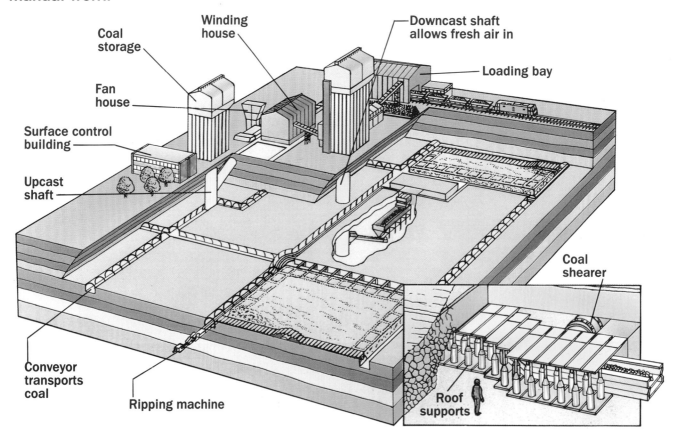

Coal storage

Winding house

Downcast shaft allows fresh air in

Loading bay

Fan house

Surface control building

Upcast shaft

Conveyor transports coal

Ripping machine

Coal shearer

Roof supports

OPEN-PIT MINING

Coal seams that occur at or near the surface can be extracted by open-pit, or strip, mining. Large, earth-moving machines strip away the overlying soil and rock, called the overburden, to reveal the coal seam. Huge excavators use giant grabs to scoop up the coal and load it into dumper trucks for transportation to the preparation plant. Draglines use cables or chains to draw buckets across the coal face. Some excavators, called bucket wheel excavators, have a large wheel rimmed with toothed buckets that dig into the seam as the wheel revolves.

Some countries have laws requiring that farm land is reclaimed after mining. After the coal has been removed, the soil is put back and the land may be returned to agriculture, or turned into parkland.

△ Uncontrolled open-pit mining can ruin agricultural land, so today the overburden is usually replaced and the land reclaimed when mining activities have finished.

POWDER AND GAS

Some of the coal that is mined for use in power plants and industry is converted to powder or gas. Powdered coal can be pumped along pipelines like a liquid, and it is easier to burn efficiently. At some mines, the coal is powdered either underground as it is being cut, or at the surface before it is pumped into tanker trucks and carried away.

In an even more advanced process, the coal can be set on fire underground to produce gas. A limited supply of oxygen is pumped down a narrow shaft to keep the fire burning in a controlled way. The fuel gas produced passes up a second pipe to the surface. The solid residue remaining is coke, which is used in iron smelting.

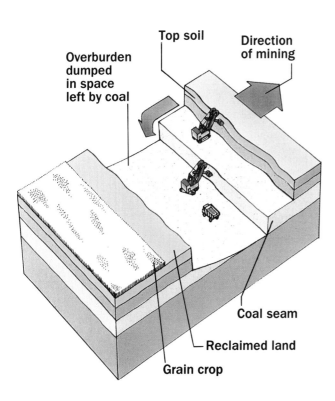

Top soil

Direction of mining

Overburden dumped in space left by coal

Coal seam

Reclaimed land

Grain crop

△ An open-pit coal mine employs large dragline excavators to remove overburden, and giant diggers to scoop away the coal.

Oil and gas, two of the most valuable natural resources, are used as fuel and in the production of synthetic materials and pharmaceuticals. They are found deep underground in porous rock, which holds them like a sponge, trapped beneath an impervious rock layer which prevents them from rising any further.

EXPLORING FOR OIL AND GAS

The sinking of an oil well is made using a rotary drill bit at the end of joined-up steel pipes called a string. A slurry of drilling fluid, known as mud, is pumped down the center of the drill, and the pressure carries mud and fragments of broken rock back to the surface. There scientists examine the rock fragments and decide on whether to sink a test well. Equipment near the top of the well can seal it off quickly in case there is a sudden blowout of oil or gas.

On land, the drilling equipment is slung from a steel derrick which straddles the hole. For offshore oil and gas wells, the drill is mounted on a rig that floats or stands on long legs that are extended to reach to the sea bottom.

△ Oil drilling rigs are among the largest structures afloat. Some are towed on their sides into position before being swung upright by flooding their buoyancy tanks.

▽ Offshore drilling rigs can reach deposits of gas and oil up to 18,500 feet below the seabed.

Drill bit and mud system
▽ The diamond-tipped bit used for drilling oil wells is hollow, so that liquid mud can be pumped down its center.

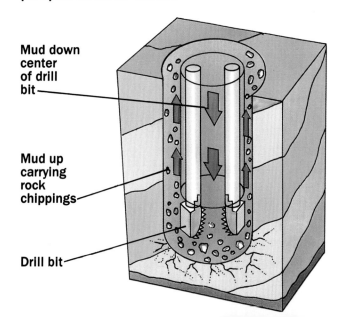

Mud down center of drill bit

Mud up carrying rock chippings

Drill bit

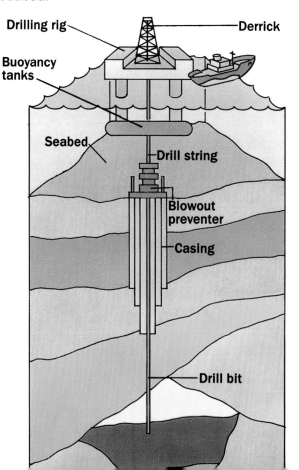

Drilling rig
Derrick
Buoyancy tanks
Seabed
Drill string
Blowout preventer
Casing
Drill bit

PRODUCTION

Once oil or gas have been discovered in commercial quantity, a production platform is set up. Wells are drilled over the whole field to increase the rate of extraction. A production platform may have up to 50 wells running into the oil field. A tool called a whipstock is used to make the drill change direction. This allows the wells to be bent very gradually up to an angle of 40 degrees. Oil pumped up through the well passes through equipment to separate the gas, water, and other impurities from the oil, which is then piped to refineries.

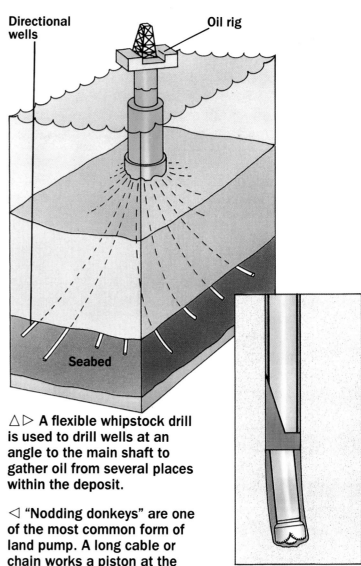

△▷ A flexible whipstock drill is used to drill wells at an angle to the main shaft to gather oil from several places within the deposit.

◁ "Nodding donkeys" are one of the most common form of land pump. A long cable or chain works a piston at the bottom of the shaft.

Whipstock

PRESSURE FOR PUMPING

To see how gas pressure can pump a liquid, cut a piece of plastic sponge to fill a plastic box. Bore two holes in a piece of balsa wood so that they are a tight fit for two drinking straws. Soak the sponge in water. Then fit the wooden lid to the box. Blow down one of the straws and note how water is forced upward out of the other straw.

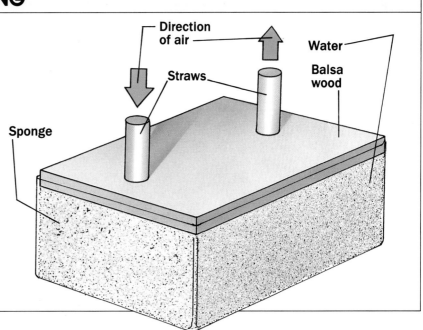

Ores are formed within the earth's crust. They are rocks that contain minerals such as metals which can be recovered economically. Gold ores are mined profitably with a low gold-to-rock ratio, because gold commands a high price. Iron, however, which is abundant, has a high iron-to-rock ratio.

△ Iron ore is one of the world's most important minerals because of the widespread use of steel, which is an alloy of iron and carbon.

FORMATION

Mineral deposits containing metal ores are created in different ways in or beneath the earth's crust. Some, like chromium, iron, and nickel, come to the surface in igneous rocks. In some places there are pools of magma which cool and form rocks, leaving a mixture of very hot water and minerals. This may react with nearby rocks and deposit minerals that can crystallize into veins of copper, lead, and zinc (1). Metals are also formed when the hot water and mineral mixture seeps into cracks (2), reacts with rocks such as limestone (3), or seeps through molten lava (4). Water trapped in the rocks may carry mineral deposits to the seabed as springs (5).

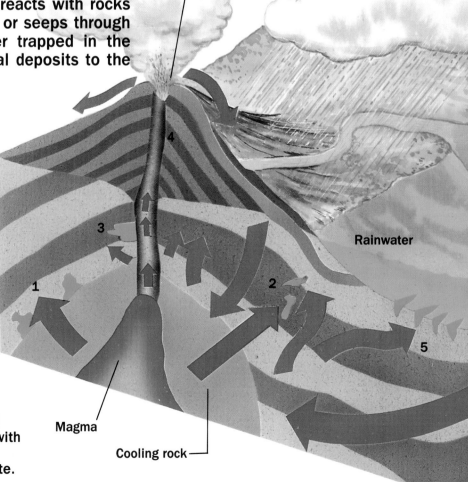

Volcano

Rainwater

Some metals, like gold and silver, do not react readily with surrounding rocks and may occur in an almost pure state.

Magma

Cooling rock

PURE METAL OR ALLOY?

Some metals are used in their pure state. Aluminum in drink cans and copper in electrical wiring are pure metals. Other objects are made from alloys, mixtures of metals with more useful properties than those of the individual components. Gunmetal, a mixture of copper, tin, and zinc, is used on ships for its strength and resistance to corrosion.

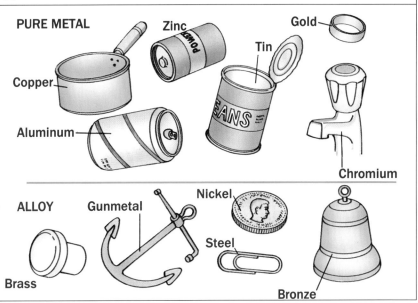

PURE METAL

Copper · Zinc · Tin · Gold · Chromium · Aluminum

ALLOY · Gunmetal · Nickel · Steel · Bronze · Brass

▽ Forced into chambers in the earth's crust, magma cools and releases mineral-rich liquid. Within these mineral "rivers," ores are created.

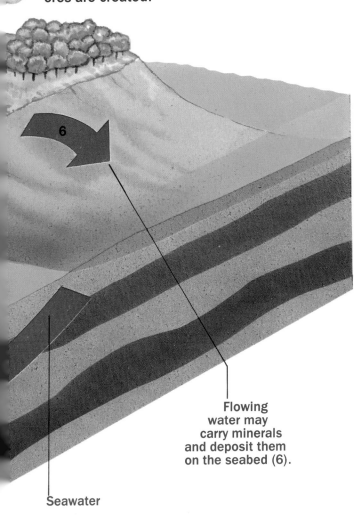

6

Seawater

Flowing water may carry minerals and deposit them on the seabed (6).

Land surface

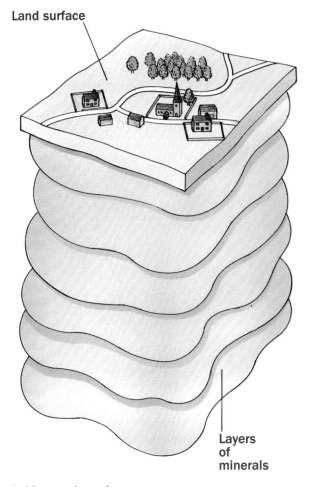

Layers of minerals

△ Many minerals are transported by water. They are deposited in rock layers. The diagram shows how the mineral deposits may look after the surrounding rock is removed.

Mining is any method of extracting ores, whether they are deep underground, or very near the surface. Surface mining is cheaper than underground mining, and for this reason underground mining is generally used only for the more valuable ores. But some valuable minerals, such as gold, are also found near the surface.

SURFACE MINING

Ores and metals washed to their locations with sediment are called placer deposits. The sediment is shoveled into a trough. Water flows down the trough, washing the sediment away and leaving the heavy ore behind. Extracting placer deposits by hand is called panning.

If the ore-bearing sediment is thick, the ore is extracted by dredging. An artificial lake is created upon which a dredger is floated. The dredger scoops up gravel and extracts the ore by washing away the sediment with streams of water.

Open-pit mining (see page 13) is also used to mine surface ore deposits in the same way as coal is extracted.

△ Panning for gold is an old method of mining that requires a lot of patience and strong muscles. Gold occurs separately as placer deposits in the gravel of streams.

▽ Copper ores are among the valuable minerals that are extracted by open-pit mining.

UNDERGROUND MINING

Metal ores are often obtained from igneous rock deep underground where they formed due to the action of cooling magma (see page 16).

The techniques for the underground mining of ores are similar to those used for mining coal (see page 12). First miners dig a shaft almost 10,000 feet deep. They then make horizontal tunnels, called levels, into the deposits of ore by drilling or, in very hard rock, by blasting with explosives. Conveyor belts or small railway cars carry the ore back to the shaft, where an elevator hauls it to the surface. Apart from being used to obtain the precious metals gold and silver, underground mining is most often used to extract copper, lead, and zinc. In some parts of the world, nickel is also obtained by underground mining.

△ Tin ores that occur as deposits mixed with thick layers of gravel or sand can be extracted by draglines.

PANNING FOR "GOLD"

Half fill a bowl with water, and put in about ten coins and a similar number of small, plastic "pretend" coins. Add two or three cupfuls of sand (1). Then take a saucer or shallow dish and scoop up some of the mixture of sand and coins. Making sure there is always some water in the saucer, swirl the mixture around in a circular motion (2). The sand and light coins are washed away, leaving behind the heavy coins in the saucer (3).

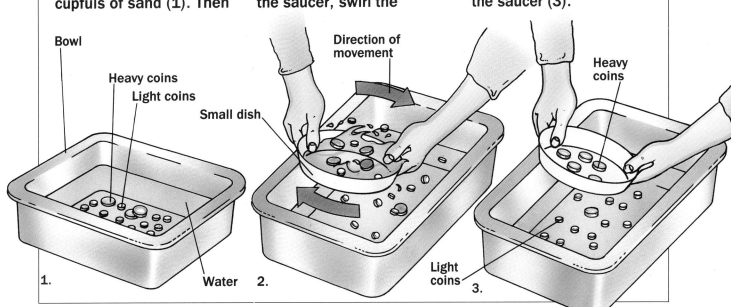

Bowl

Heavy coins

Light coins

Small dish

Direction of movement

Heavy coins

1.

Water 2.

Light coins 3.

An ore consists of a metal combined chemically with elements such as oxygen or sulfur to produce oxides and sulfides. Refining is the means of extracting the metal from its ore, and includes smelting, which involves heat and often additional substances, and electrolysis, whereby electricity breaks down the ore.

SMELTING

Some ores, such as an oxide of copper, can be smelted using heat alone. But most need a more complex chemical reaction. Iron ore is smelted by mixing it with lime and coke. The mixture is heated to a high temperature in a blast furnace. Molten iron sinks to the bottom, and impurities, chiefly silicon, combine with the lime to make "slag" which floats to the top.

Iron from a blast furnace, known as "pig iron," is made into steel in a furnace called a converter. Pig iron and lime are melted and oxygen blasted through to reduce the amount of carbon in the pig iron. Lime combines with the remaining impurities to form slag. Steel is poured off and cast into ingots.

△ Iron is smelted in a blast furnace. The molten metal is tapped off from the bottom of the furnace and run into molds as pig iron.

▽ Iron from a blast furnace may go straight into steel-making. In the basic oxygen process, in which lime is added to pig iron, impurities in the metal are oxidized and escape as gases or accumulate as slag.

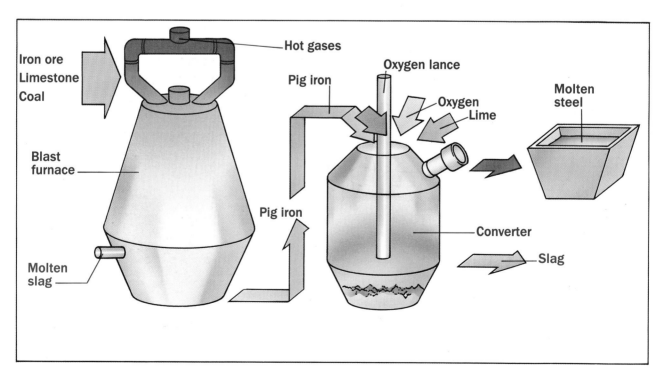

Iron ore
Limestone
Coal

Hot gases

Pig iron

Oxygen lance

Oxygen
Lime

Molten steel

Blast furnace

Pig iron

Converter

Molten slag

Slag

ELECTROLYSIS

Electrolysis is the breaking down and recombining of a substance in its pure form by electricity. Solid compounds are dissolved in water or melted so that molecules are free to move, making mineral extraction possible.

Copper is one such mineral that can be extracted by electrolysis. Crushed copper ore is dissolved in sulfuric acid forming a solution of copper sulfate. A direct current is passed through this solution via conducting plates called electrodes. Attracted to a negative charge, pure copper splits from the rest of the dissolved material and collects on the negative electrode as pure copper.

△ In the electrolytic extraction of aluminum, the bauxite ore (aluminum oxide) is melted with cryolite (an aluminum fluoride).

ELECTROLYSIS EXPERIMENT

Ask your teacher to help you to make a weak solution of copper sulfate in a jar or beaker. Use crocodile clips to join wires to a copper coin and a "silver" coin. Connect the other ends of the wires to a battery — the copper coin (anode) to the positive terminal and the "silver" coin (cathode) to the negative terminal. Pure copper moves from the copper to the "silver" coin.

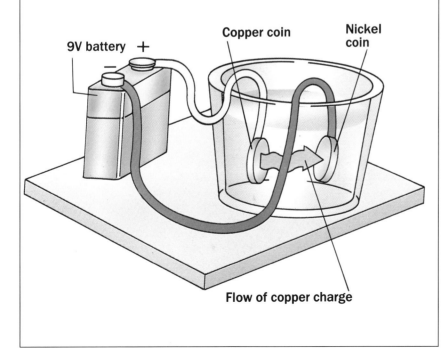

9V battery   +

Copper coin

Nickel coin

Flow of copper charge

DID YOU KNOW?

Mercury is the only metal that is liquid at room temperature. Its ore (mercury sulfide) is smelted by heating it with a stream of hot air or oxygen. The impure metal is purified using distillation. This process involves heating the impure metal until it forms a vapor, and then cooling the vapor to make it reform pure liquid metal.

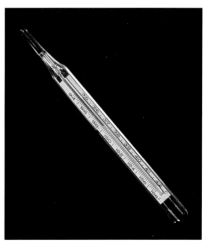

Nonmetallic minerals are among our oldest resources. These include asbestos, mica, and talc. Some occur as salts such as table salt, gypsum and potash. Carbon and sulfur often occur in a pure state. We still rely on nonmetallic minerals today, from crockery to space shuttle ceramic insulating tiles.

FORMATION

Most nonmetallic minerals occur in sedimentary rocks. These are formed when particles of other rocks, broken down by weathering, accumulate as sediments at the bottoms of lakes and seas, and are changed by pressure. Clay and limestone, for instance, are sedimentary rocks that are quarried as minerals. Salt from dried-up lakes and seas is an important nonmetallic mineral also found underground. Evaporation of salt water can also give rise to precipitation deposits of minerals such as anhydrite and gypsum (forms of calcium sulfate) and potash.

Sulfur is a nonmetallic mineral that occurs at the surface near volcanoes, or underground in areas with oil deposits.

△ Sulfur occurs at the surface near volcanic activity, such as in these hot sulfur springs.

▽ Machinery at a quarry (left) crushes rock to make gravel for road-building. The excavator (right) scoops up gypsum for making plaster.

EXTRACTION

Like metallic ores, most nonmetallic minerals are extracted by digging them out of the ground. Near the surface, minerals such as gravel and sand are obtained by quarrying. Open-pit mining can also be used. Salt deposits can be mined, although in hot countries most of it is now produced by the evaporation of seawater from shallow pools.

Sulfur lying deep underground is extracted by a method called the Frasch process. Engineers sink three pipes into the sulfur deposit. Hot water sent down the outer pipe melts the sulfur, which is forced to the surface by air pumped down the central pipe.

△ For centuries people have extracted salt from seawater. The water is trapped in pools called pans, and the salt left to crystallize as the sun's heat makes water evaporate.

MINERAL	HOW EXTRACTED	MINERAL	HOW EXTRACTED
Salt	Salt is mined or extracted from seawater.	Sulfur	Sulfur is mined or extracted from oil and gas.
Quartz	Quartz, a crystalline form of silica, is mined.	Graphite	Graphite is a form of carbon that is mined.
Borax	Borax (for making heat-resistant glass) is mined.	Gypsum	Open-pit gypsum is used for chalk and plaster.

SALT AND EVAPORATION

You can make your own salt-extraction plant. Dissolve as much salt as possible in a glass or jar of hot water and put the glass in a warm place — such as a sunny window sill. The heat causes the water to evaporate while the salt stays behind, appearing as crystals in the glass. The size of the crystals depends on the rate of evaporation.

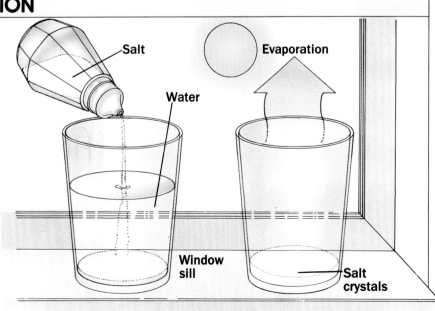

Many minerals occur in the form of crystals. Some, because of their color, beauty and rarity, have been highly valued since ancient times as gems or semiprecious stones. The most valuable are diamond, emerald, ruby, and sapphire. Pearls, formed from nacre inside oysters, are also precious stones.

HOW GEMS ARE FORMED

When magma from the earth's core pushes toward the crust it solidifies at about 2,012°F, creating igneous rock. If this happens slowly, large mineral crystals will form within the rock. If exposed, surface erosion eats the rock away and these potentially gem-bearing sediments are washed into waterways.

Gems also form where the earth's crust folds into mountains, or magma helps to reforge sedimentary rock into metamorphic rock. When limestone changes into marble, aluminum in the limestone may recrystallize with silica to form rubies or sapphires.

Not all magma is the same and its texture, chemistry, and density determine the type of gemstone it will form, if any are formed at all.

△ Sapphires glisten among other precious stones in a piece of gem-bearing rock.

▽ The buckling earth forms mountain peaks from which gem-bearing sediments eventually spill into valleys below. Carried by rain water the gems end up in distant riverbeds, lakes and oceans.

Emerald is deposited in veins of metamorphic rock.

Sapphire and ruby

Hot springs

Garnet and jade formed in solid rock.

Tourmaline and zircon are formed beneath volcanoes.

Molten granite

Earthquakes

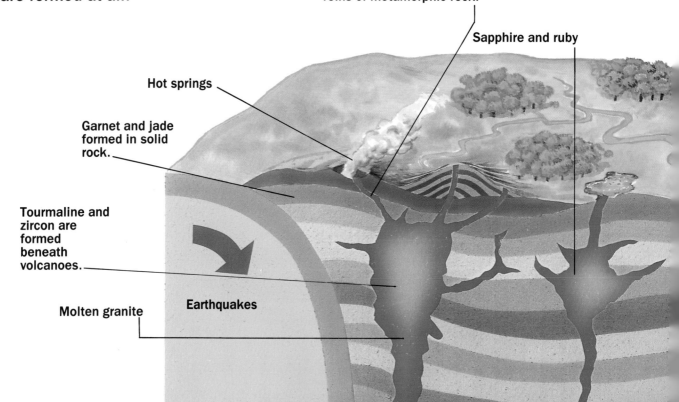

GROW YOUR OWN CRYSTALS

Put some hot (but not boiling) water into a jar or beaker and add soap powder that contains sodium carbonate until no more will dissolve.

Support a button on a length of cotton in it. As the solution evaporates over several days, soda will begin to form a mass of crystals on the button.

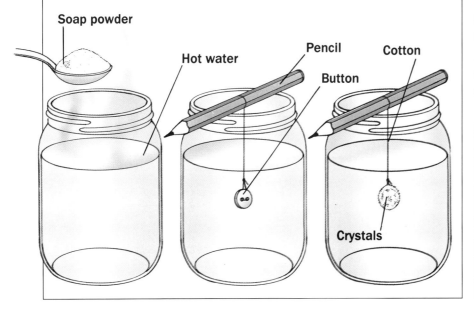

Soap powder

Hot water

Pencil

Cotton

Button

Crystals

Diamond is a form of the element carbon, as are the black substances graphite and charcoal. It is the hardest natural substance in the world. Gem-quality diamonds consist of pure transparent crystals, which are rare. Most diamonds are discolored and used as industrial abrasives. Coal is another mineral that consists mainly of carbon.

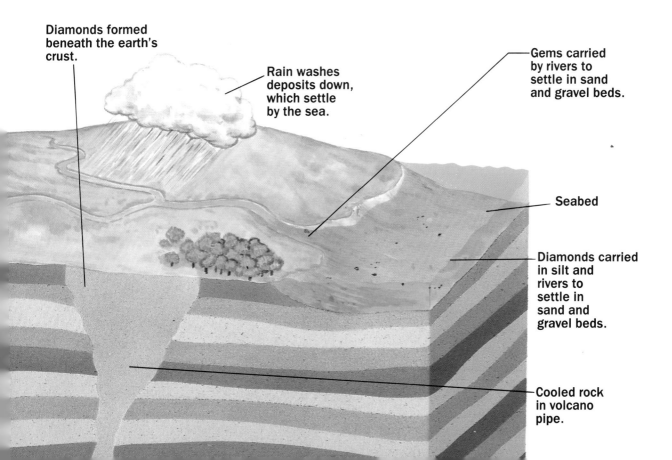

Diamonds formed beneath the earth's crust.

Rain washes deposits down, which settle by the sea.

Gems carried by rivers to settle in sand and gravel beds.

Seabed

Diamonds carried in silt and rivers to settle in sand and gravel beds.

Cooled rock in volcano pipe.

Gemstones are mined using most of the methods employed for extracting ores (see pages 18-19). Mining is difficult, however, because gems tend to lie within hard rocks. Also, because gems are rare, many tons of rock have to be dug out, crushed, and sorted to find only a few stones of gem quality.

A LARGE DIAMOND MINE

Large mines are constructed to extract diamonds from the "pipe" of rock, called blue ground, that once formed the vent of a volcano. At first open-pit mining methods can be used, with giant excavators to dig out the blue ground. But as the hole gets deeper and deeper, vertical shafts and horizontal tunnels have to be built. Often the rock is crushed underground before being lifted to the surface for sorting. The crushed rock passes along conveyor belts under strong lights while workers pick out the gems. On average, even in a rich African mine, 14 tons of rock must be dug to produce only one gram of precious diamonds.

IDENTIFYING GEMS

Most gems have characteristic colors: blue aquamarine and sapphire, green emerald and turquoise, yellow — or the rarer blue — topaz, purple amethyst and red ruby. Jade varies in color from white to green, brown orange or, rarely, lilac. Precious opal is iridescent and multicolored.

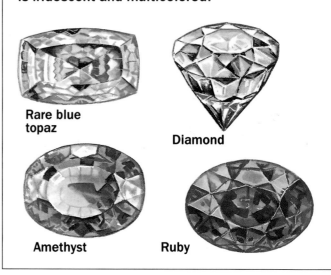

Rare blue topaz

Diamond

Amethyst

Ruby

▽ Excavators have dug out tons of rock in the search for diamonds at an open-pit mine in Southern Africa.

Main shaft

Open-pit mine

Collapsing rock

Mining level tunnel

Crusher

Blue ground

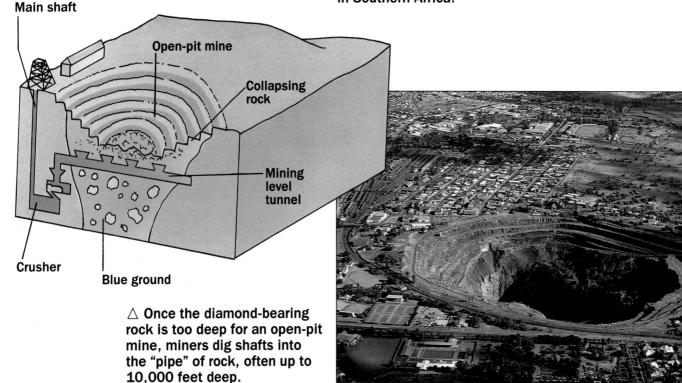

△ Once the diamond-bearing rock is too deep for an open-pit mine, miners dig shafts into the "pipe" of rock, often up to 10,000 feet deep.

Aquamarine

Sapphire

Emerald

Turquoise

Jade

Opal

Diamonds are weighed in carats (1 carat equals 200 milligrams). The largest raw diamond ever found, the Cullinan, weighed 3,106 carats (21-9 ounces) before it was cut into smaller stones. One of these, the Star of Africa, weighs more than 530 carats (3.5 ounces).

OPAL MINES

Opals are unusual multicoloured gems consisting mainly of silica (the same mineral that forms sand). They do not form crystals, but are found as irregular lumps in rock cavities. Most come from Australia, where they are obtained from open-pit mines or from underground tunnels that follow the opal seams.

▽ The entrance to an opal mine may be merely a hole in the ground, with a simple crane to lower the miners.

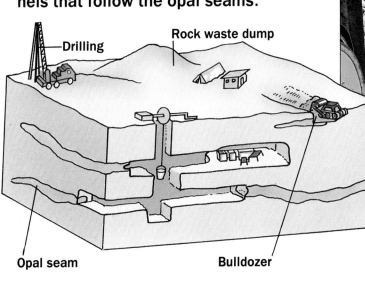

Rock waste dump

Drilling

Opal seam

Bulldozer

◁ Opals are formed in seams and may be mined at the surface or underground. The most valuable are the black opals that are found in New South Wales, Australia.

Recycling and resource conservation will help us to make the planet's dwindling supply of minerals last. We can also use technology to create substitutes for non-renewable resources. The metals we use can also be recycled. Scientists are looking to develop a synthetic fuel to replace decreasing oil supplies.

RECYCLING

One way everybody can help to conserve mineral resources is by recycling manufactured goods to reuse the materials they are made from. At home, scrap metal (mainly food and beverage cans) and glass bottles can be separated from paper, plastics and food waste. Some have built recycling plants for processing domestic and industrial waste. In addition to saving materials, recycling also saves the energy — and therefore fuel — that goes into extracting and refining various minerals. For example, recyling aluminum only uses about five percent of the energy required to separate it from ore in the first place.

△ Glass bottles and jars put into a collection bin can be recycled, thus saving mineral resources and the energy used in making new glass.

SCRAP METAL

Steel and aluminum are the chief metals used in the world, and the most frequently discarded. But these metals, along with iron, tin, and copper, are also the most easily recycled. Every year millions of cars, each containing a ton of steel, end up in scrap yards. This scrap can be put through a crusher and reused for making new steel.

Food and beverage cans also yield valuable scrap from the billions produced worldwide each year. If collected and recycled, this scrap can be recrafted into new cans, saving both metal and energy.

◁ Scrapped cars account for millions of tons of waste steel. They can be crushed into blocks of scrap and used in making more steel.

SYNTHETICS

Some mineral resources can be conserved by using man-made substitutes, which may be cheaper than the natural substances. Artificial diamonds, made by subjecting carbon to tremendous heat and pressure, are employed as abrasives and cutting agents. Imitation diamonds, such as the man-made mineral yttrium iron garnet (YIG), are used in jewelry. Some synthetic materials, such as plastics, consume mineral resources and so should be recycled wherever possible.

△ Artificial diamonds are just as hard as natural ones and are used in industry for making saws, drills, and other kinds of cutting tools.

△ A biogas generator, also called a digester, consumes vegetable wastes to produce a continuous supply of methane for use as a fuel.

ALTERNATIVE GAS

Scientists estimate that supplies of natural gas could run out within the next 100 years. But methane, the principle gas in natural gas, can be tapped from a variety of other sources. Methane is produced when organic matter decays in the absence of air. So it is possible to harvest plants which can be processed for methane. The basic process is fermentation, also used to make alcohol (for fuel) from wood, particularly in Brazil.

▽ Waste from a nuclear power plant being moved by rail in crashproof containers, on its way to a reprocessing plant.

REPROCESSING

Reprocessing helps to turn dangerously radioactive spent uranium fuel into material suitable for new fuel rods used in nuclear reactors. The old fuel rods are cooled and dissolved in acid. Unused uranium can then be extracted. To ensure safety, the procedure is carried out by remote control with operators shielded behind thick protective walls. In recovering and reusing uranium, reprocessing reduces hazardous high-level waste.

In the future, people may seek minerals beyond the boundaries of the earth, mining the moon, asteroids or other planets. Previously inaccessable mineral store-houses on earth may also be exploited as we push the frontiers of technology at home. For instance, ocean beds may one day be tapped economically.

Drawing of a proposed mine on a moon of Mars.

Machine for collecting nodules on the seabed.

Oil shales and tar sands are porous sedimentary rocks that have soaked up thick crude oil, as a sponge might soak up water. Shales can be excavated, or the oil melted and piped to the surface by pumping in superheated steam. But the latter is not yet cost efficient.

Potato-sized nodules of minerals containing the metal manganese have been found in deep water on the bed of the Pacific Ocean. The nodules also contain cobalt and nickel. It may become possible in future for remote-controlled submersible machines to gather the nodules and take them to the surface.

Another future possibility is the use of remote-controlled "platforms" on the seabed to drill for small deposits of gas or oil that cannot be extracted economically from the surface.

A dragline excavator mining tar sands.

Biogas
A gas, consisting mainly of methane, made by fermenting vegetable waste, used in place of precious mineral sources of natural gas.

Crude oil
A major fossil fuel mineral consisting of a sticky liquid mixture of hydrocarbons, also known as petroleum.

Electrolysis
A chemical reaction brought about by an electric current. Typically a salt, either in solution or in its molten state, is decomposed into its component elements.

Fossil fuel
Any mineral, based on carbon, extracted for use as a fuel, such as coal, oil, or natural gas.

Hydrocarbon
A chemical compound of hydrogen and carbon, like oil and natural gas.

Magma
The molten rock that lies just below the earth's crust.

Mineral
A substance of more or less constant chemical composition that is obtained from the earth.

Natural gas
A mixture of hydrocarbon gases that occurs in the earth's crust, often associated with deposits of crude oil.

Nodule
A rounded lump of something. A few metallic minerals occur as nodules on the seabed.

Open-pit mine
A type of mine whose minerals can be extracted (once any overlying soil or rock is removed) by digging down in "steps" using excavators.

Ore
A mineral that contains enough metal (usually as one of its chemical compounds) to be worth mining.

Petroleum
Another name for crude oil.

Placer deposit
A deposit of an ore that has become concentrated in one place, usually by the action of flowing water.

Recycling
A method of saving resources by re-using the materials in discarded goods.

Refining
The extraction of metals from their ores, or of purifying metals after smelting.

Rock
Any of the mineral substances that the earth is made of, usually meaning the solid substances at the surface of the earth and in the earth's crust.

Slurry
A fluid mixture of a powdered solid and a liquid (usually water), such as the thin mud used in oil wells.

Smelting
Method of obtaining metals from their ores using heat, and usually involving mixing the ore with other substances.

Strip mine
A type of mine in which minerals are extracted at the surface using excavators. Typically used of surface coal mines, whereas "open-pit" usually refers to a metal mine.

Photographic Credits:
Cover and pages 8 top and bottom, 9 bottom, 13, 14, 18 top, 23 and 26: Robert Harding Picture Library; pages 5, 15, 18 bottom, 19, 22 top, 24 and 29 middle: The Hutchison Library; pages 10, 12, 16, 21 bottom, 22 bottom left, 25 and 29 top: Science Photo Library; pages 11 and 22 bottom right: Bruce Coleman Limited; pages 20 and 27 top and bottom: Frank Spooner Pictures; pages 28 top and bottom: Paul Nightingale; page 29 bottom: British Nuclear Fuels Limited.